The
Home Seller's
Guide
Preparing Your Home
for Sale

by Christina Vaughan

ISBN 978-0-9641697-0-8

Castlebrook Publications
1535 Farmers Lane, PMB #237
Santa Rosa, CA 95405
www.castlebrookbooks.com

TABLE OF CONTENTS

Introduction

In many areas of the country these days, the housing market is a buyer's market. Sellers may wait several months before they get a buyer, or just give up the idea of moving all together.

Even if that is the case in your area, there's no reason why your home can't be one that sells—and at a satisfactory price in a short amount of time. But in order for your home to sell, you may have to make an extra effort to outdo the competition.

You've probably already spent nearly all the money you can to fix it up. However, if you can squeeze out a little more, and do some rearranging and cleaning up, you can save yourself months of anxiety, and get a better price for your home.

Maybe you love your home the way it is, and you don't see why someone else wouldn't love it just as much. It's probably a very nice home, but there may be some things that detract from its beauty that you don't notice because you've gotten used to them; or some things that, while not inherently unattractive, take the potential buyers' attention away from the home itself.

Assuming you have already painted your house inside and out, (if you haven't, you'd better grab a paint brush) and done all the landscaping and decorating you can afford, there are still innumerable small things that may need doing, which added up, can keep your house on the market longer, and longer, and longer.

So, let's get down to business, because that's what it is—a business transaction. You want to make a sale. Your Realtor or agent, you may say, is supposed to do that. But Realtors and agents can only do so much. They can bring people to look, but it's your product and you're the only one who can enhance it.

The First Impression

The prospective buyer's first impression of the house is formed at the curb, even before they get out of the car. I can't emphasize too strongly that the first impression the potential buyer has is the absolute, most important, number one factor in her liking the house. I say "her" because usually, though not always, a man and a woman buy a house together. If the woman doesn't like it, the answer will almost always be no. If you are a single male owner, you should pay particular attention to this because your house probably doesn't have much of a woman's touch in it. You may want to consider having a sister or a woman friend go through this Guide with you and help you with some feminine touches.

Viewing your home through the eyes of a buyer

We are going to walk through your house and go over every detail, one room at a time. We are going to include the garage, the yard, and the neighbor's yard. And we will begin at the curb. Take this book out there with you now and start checking off what needs to be done as we go. Note pages are included throughout the book for you to write down details and creative ideas you will get once you start looking. Pretend you are a buyer and you haven't seen your house before. Give it your most critical eye.

At the Curb

1 □   Is your house readily available for viewing? If you don't want to have a lock box on your house, can you have a friend or neighbor be there for appointments if you can't be? The harder it is to see your home, the more likely it is that potential buyers will be looking at another house and buying it instead of yours.

2 □   Is the mailbox at the curb rusty or dented? Is the post half-eaten by termites or bent out of shape by a run-in with a car? Paint, fix, replace it—whatever it takes.

3 □   Is the grass cut and are the edges trimmed?

4 □   Maybe it's only weeds and you can't afford a lawn, but is it green?

5 □   Unless it's a rustic setting where leaves are a plus, are the leaves raked up?

6 □   Are there flowers anywhere? (If it's the dead of winter in a snowstorm, you can do without them.) If not, go down to the nursery and get a few planters, dirt, and flowering plants and put some near the entrance. Take a few minutes to arrange them to look attractive.

7 □   Are there any dead bushes or plants? Take them out. You don't have to replace them if your yard looks nice without them.

8 □   Is there trash, old newspapers, dog poop, broken toys? Unbroken toys? Garden hoses waiting to be tripped over? Pick it all up and put it (or throw it) away.

9 ☐ Do you have to fight branches of trees and/or shrubs all the way down the walk? Prune them.

10 ☐ If it's been snowing, are your walks and driveways clear?

11 ☐ Do you have big cracks in driveways or concrete walks? If they are too big to patch, throw some seeds of alyssum or other low-growing flowering plants in there with a little compost and water them. Just a few here and there will do.

12 ☐ Are there big oil stains on the driveway or the garage floor? Use a driveway cleaner available at hardware stores.

13 ☐ If your neighbor's yard is an eyesore, maybe you could tell them you are trying to sell your house and every little bit helps. Maybe they wouldn't mind if you volunteered to clean it up. If it is tenant occupied, contact the landlord directly. Many cities and counties have ordinances prohibiting tall grass or weeds, or even weeds with airborne seeds (dandelions, for instance). If you have to resort to it, you can call the city or county to file a complaint.

14 ☐ If there are any cars parked on the street that obviously don't run and are eyesores, you can call the police and report them. Many cities and counties have laws about vehicles parked for over 72 hours on public streets and will tow them away.

15 ☐ What about your own vehicles? Keep them washed and waxed, and preferably in the garage. Don't leave a lot of junk in your truck bed or in your car.

Notes — At the Curb

THE FRONT OF THE HOUSE

1 ☐ Maybe you can't afford a new roof, but you can have obviously missing shingles replaced. It's one thing for a roof inspector to say the house needs a new roof, but it's even worse to see gaping holes.

2 ☐ Is the color of your house attractive? Does it harmonize with its surroundings, yet stand out as one of the most attractive houses on the block? Drive around your neighborhood. Which house would you prefer? What color is it?

3 ☐ Is your garage door closed? No matter how beautiful and tidy the inside of your garage, having the door open detracts from the looks of your home from the outside. (If your house looks better with the garage door open, you'd better do something about fixing the door.)

4 ☐ Are your screens rusted, torn, bent? If so, remove them. The house looks better without them anyway. If you don't want to replace them now, you can agree to provide them once you've got a buyer. If you live in a buggy area, you'd better replace the screens. Flies buzzing around your prospective buyer is not good. If the frames are good, you can call a screen service to come to your house and put new screen in the frames.

5 ☐ Decorative shutters on the outside of front windows could enhance the look of your home. You can purchase prepainted shutters from home improvement stores.

6 ☐ A front door looks better without a screen, so unless it's a painted wood-frame screen that matches your front door, remove it and put it in the garage. Shut the door to keep the insects out.

7 ☐ The front entrance is not the place to have peeling paint. If you paint nowhere else, paint here if it needs it—the door and trim at least.

8 ☐ Does the weather stripping on the door need replacing? (See "In General," #5.)

9 ☐ If you are painting the outside of an entry door, consider a contrasting color—for example, deep red with a gray house with white trim. Many paint stores have computers on which you can view many styles of houses and color combinations.

10 ☐ Dirt and cobwebs? They must go.

11 ☐ Is the light fixture by the door clean? Does it work? There is a light, isn't there? If not, don't let buyers come over at night. Better yet, install an attractive fixture.)

12 ☐ A doormat will help keep dirt from being tracked in, but it should clean and new.

13 ☐ Does the doorbell work? If you don't have one, do you have a knocker or a handbell (or at the very least, a sign that says "knock loud!"?
Otherwise, you may not hear potential buyers, and they may be annoyed because they think you are there for the appointment.

14 ☐ Open the front door and go in. If the door squeaks, oil the hinges and clean off any rust as best you can.

NOTES – THE FRONT OF THE HOUSE

The Entrance Hall

1 ☐ Is your entrance hall small and dark? Be sure the light is on, even in the daytime. This goes for the other rooms in your home, too, which do not get sufficient light from windows to make them cheerful and inviting. Some eye catcher at the end of the hall (a framed print or a wall hanging) or a colorful rug on the floor will draw the viewer's attention from less attractive aspects. This is a good place to have an eye-catching light fixture.

2 ☐ Hang tasteful prints, paintings, or other wall decorations here, as well as throughout the house, but nothing that will totally distract the potential buyer from noticing the good things about your house. A Realtor friend of mine told me of one house in which the owner had a family pictorial genealogy chart on the wall. People who came to see the house were so intrigued by seeing who looked like whom that they forgot about the house.

Your Living Areas

1 ☐ Do your living areas have a warm, comfortable ambience about them? Would a buyer feel at home? What you want is moderation. You don't want your home looking like either a museum or a junkyard. People should be able to walk through your home without feeling like they collected dust, or fear leaving a speck of dust behind. Consider removing delicate expensive breakables from your coffee table or any other place people may fear bumping into. Simple, uncluttered elegance is much more effective.

2 ☐ Live plants are a nice touch, but they must be well cared for and should not crowd the room.

3 ☐ On a cold day, a fire in the fireplace is warm and inviting, but don't leave it burning if you aren't home.

4 ☐ Try adding some color and cheer with colorful pillows, area rugs or window coverings. Look through home magazines to get ideas for a more updated look. *Woman's Day*, among others, has a special decorating publication with low-cost ways to achieve a decorator look.

5 ☐ If your drapes are stained or raggedy-looking, replace them. For minimal cost and effort, you can use attractive sheets. Most of them have a ready-made "rod pocket" you can remove the side stitching from and slip a rod through. You don't even have to hem them—you can leave them luxuriously over-long. Figure 1 1/2 to 2 times the width of your window for the overall curtain width. The width of the sheets is on the package and you probably won't need more than two sheets per window because of the many sizes sheets come in.

6 ☐ If your rods have rings that are open in the back, and you use cotton/polyester sheets that don't fray, you can cut little slits in the top of the sheet and slip them right onto the rings. If the rings aren't open, you can put fabric ribbon through the slits and tie the drape to the rings— tie bows or leave the ribbon long like streamers. If you have traverse rods and don't use pinch-pleated drapes, you may have to help the drapes along with your hand when you close them. You can also sew pinch-pleat tape on the top and use regular drapery hooks if you want to work harder (visit a fabric store for details).

7 ☐ Don't use clear plastic protective covers for your lampshades and furniture. It will look like the back room of a furniture store. Unless the weather's terrible, don't cover your floors with vinyl runners, either.

8 ☐   If your sofa has seen better days, consider covering it with colorful sheets. You can either sew together as many as you need to cover it, or simply tuck them in around the seat and let them hang to the floor over the sides, back, and front of the couch. If your couch is against the wall, the sheet doesn't have to hang to the floor in the back—just so it covers whatever part you see.

9 ☐   Use pillow cases to cover throw pillows. You can tie them closed with fabric ponytail holders or pretty ribbon. You can also buy ready-made, inexpensive furniture slip covers from many mail order catalogs.

10 ☐   It will be obvious no matter what you do if your floor coverings need replacing, but that's no reason for your floors to look ugly. A few attractive Oriental or Indian design rugs, strategically placed, will add to the warmth of your home. If someone loves your home and feels good in it, they will at least get to the bargaining table. Maybe you are willing to reduce the price a little because the floor coverings need replacing, but you've got to have a prospect to negotiate with. Since new rugs can be expensive, and rugs like these sometimes have an added charm with a little wear, try the private ads for used furniture and accessories. You can even use such rugs as wall hangings.

11 ☐   If you have hardwood floors, wax and polish them.

12 ☐   Get rid of all clutter—newspapers, coats, shoes, video cassettes, dirty glasses, etc. A few attractive magazines around—decorating magazines, for instance—or a book or two, are fine. Just don't make them so interesting that somebody reads them instead of looking at your house.

13 ☐   Clutter can also include too much furniture. Are your rooms so crowded you can't walk through them easily? They will look more spacious with perhaps a little less furniture.

14 ☐   Don't set your dining tale for an imaginary dinner. It will look like a china store instead of a home. A vase of flowers, preferably live, will suffice. If your dining table is in poor condition, you could get a lovely fabric remnant on sale (maybe sew two pieces together to hang to the floor all around if that works for you) to cover it. If the loose threads are trimmed, you don't even have to hem it.

15 ☐   Are the rooms and furniture vacuumed and dusted?

16 ☐   If the rock or brick around your fireplace is stained, clean it with an acid-based cleaner available at paint and hardware stores.

Notes — Entrance/Living Areas

_____ _____

_____ _____

_____ _____

_____ _____

_____ _____

_____ _____

_____ _____

_____ _____

_____ _____

_____ _____

_____ _____

_____ _____

_____ _____

_____ _____

_____ _____

The Kitchen

1 ☐ *Clean and shining?* That's what it should be. Don't leave dirty dishes anywhere, not even in the sink. Remove hardwater stains on ceramic sinks with pumice stone. Bleach is also helpful. (Open the windows while you're at it, and be sure to follow caution statements on bleach bottles.)

2 ☐ Don't use a steel scouring pad on your sinks, ceramic or steel. It leaves scratches that stains become more imbedded in as time goes by. Remove stubborn stains from counter tops with a gentle scouring powder such as Bon Ami.

3 ☐ Is the floor clean enough to eat off of? Bon Ami may also remove floor stains you thought wouldn't come out.

4 ☐ An attractive, washable throw rug might be effective here, but be sure to keep it clean.

5 ☐ Dried flowers, live flowers, or bowls of *real* fruit are attractive accents, as are some kitchen utensils and gadgets, but use them sparingly.

6 ☐ Don't clutter up your counters. You want potential buyers to see how much counter space you have and how much fun it will be to cook in this kitchen.

7 ☐ Clean your stove inside and out. A greasy drawer in the bottom is a no-no. And never put contact paper in it. The heat from the oven will melt the glue and make a mess when you or someone else tries to remove it.

8 □ Remove *everything* from the front and sides of your refrigerator. The only exception to this rule is if the paint is in terrible shape. Then, put up the nicest children's artwork you can find. Clean it, inside and out until it sparkles.

9 □ Clean all appliance fronts, tops, and insides, including the range hood and filter. If your refrigerator has a drip pan under it, clean it out so it won't be a source of smelly mold.

10 □ Don't leave food in your garbage disposal. Run lemon peels through it to keep your sink smelling fresh.

11 □ Clean cabinet fronts, ceilings and walls to remove grease and soot build-up. Clean out cabinets and keep them orderly. Take out the garbage *every* day so odors don't accumulate.

12 □ Brown, harvest gold, and olive green appliances are outdated. Replace them if you can. The kitchen can be one of the most important selling features of a house.

13 □ For as little as $25 you can easily improve the look of your kitchen by changing the cabinet door handles and drawer pulls. Hardware stores carry a wide variety of styles.

14 □ If you want to upgrade the cabinets, you can get them refaced with new doors and drawer fronts. It's less expensive than replacing the entire cabinets.

15 □ You can have laminated countertops relaminated rather than replacing them.

NOTES – THE KITCHEN

Bedrooms

1 ☐   Are the beds made, are the covers attractive?

2 ☐   Raggedy posters in children's rooms should be removed, and any holes patched and the walls painted.

3 ☐   Clothes, shoes, toys, and trash should be put where they belong.

4 ☐   Unless you have a room exclusively for exercise equipment, store it out of sight. It's not charming, may take up too much room, and it may project negative images of sweat and struggle when what you want is an image of comfort and rest.

5 ☐   Closets should be kept neat and orderly. It's a good time to clean them out and get rid of what you don't use any longer. The paint in the closet should look as nice as the rest of the house. Clean floors, and no cobwebs or dust. Kids' toys can go in colorful plastic stacking baskets, laundry baskets—even cardboard boxes are preferable to a heap of toys tossed on the floor.

Bathrooms

1 ☐   They should be as sparkling clean as possible.

2 ☐   Fix leaky faucets, showerheads and toilets. Keep plungers put away. Putting them next to the toilet leaves an impression that they are needed all the time. If they are, call a service to clean out all your drains. People will flush your toilets and run water in the sinks to see if all works well.

3 ☐   Replace stained shower curtains.

4 ☐ Remove stained bathroom caulking around tubs, floors, and sinks, and replace it. It's not hard to do, just follow the directions on the tube.

5 ☐ Remove mildew stains from grout with a mildew cleaner or bleach. Regular cleansers are usually not strong enough.

6 ☐ Pumice stone can be used to remove hardwater stains from your toilets and other ceramic fixtures. You can try bleach, too, if necessary. It doesn't get rid of the residue as the pumice does, just bleaches it.

7 ☐ Wash the floors around toilets frequently. Urine quickly turns to ammonia and creates a powerful odor. Wash rugs near toilets often.

8 ☐ Shower door tracks should be scrubbed inside and out. A toothbrush is effective for this purpose.

9 ☐ Keep the bathroom door open when not in use. This goes for shower doors and curtains, too. Mildew proliferates in a closed, damp environment. Use the fan when showering and leave it on awhile afterwards, or open the window.

10 ☐ Provide clean towels often. Fold and arrange them neatly. Don't leave wet towels lying around.

11 ☐ Clean the insides of medicine cabinets and other cabinets and keep them orderly. Throw out useless, outdated items. Keep waste baskets clean and empty them often. Keep toothbrushes in a clean holder or in the medicine cabinet. Keep all grooming items clean put away when not in use. In other words, *no clutter.*

12 ☐ Keep the knick-knacks clean, and use them sparingly so that counters look more spacious.

Notes — Bedrooms and Bathrooms

Garages, Attics, and Basements

1 ☐   Get rid of the junk and trash. The garage should be empty enough to fit the number of cars it's supposed to hold. If you have a lot to store, you may want to rent a storage space instead of storing it in the garage.

2 ☐   Tools can be hung on the wall. Hooks and hangers of many kinds, as well as pegboard, can be obtained at hardware stores. You can put up a couple of shelves to neatly store things.

3 ☐   Vacuum and dust. These rooms are a spider's haven, so get rid of the cobwebs often.

4 ☐   Make sure the outside of furnaces, water heaters, and air conditioners are clean—if they are in closets, clean those as well.

5 ☐   Hang neat and clean washable curtains over windows. Wash them often. This is not the time to hang old rags over these windows, or even dust collectors like blinds. You want your garage, attic, or basement to look like a pleasant place for a workshop, a ping-pong table, or a laundry room.

6 ☐   Be sure they are well lit. An unusable attic, however, probably doesn't have or need any lights.

7 ☐   Paint the walls in usable spaces of these rooms.

8 ☐   This is the perfect time for a yard or garage sale. If these rooms are filled to the ceiling with things you never use, people may feel a little uncomfortable at the possibility that this stuff might still be here after you move out.

Involve your kids in the sale. They probably have plenty of clothes and toys pouring out of their closets that they have outgrown. They will be more interested in cleaning out their rooms if they can get money for their castoffs. They can sell cookies or doughnuts at the sale, too. Don't forget the lemonade and the coffee.

NOTES — GARAGES, ATTICS, AND BASEMENTS

THE BACKYARD

1 ☐   Whatever vegetation you have should be green (unless it's supposed to be some other color), trimmed, and watered.

2 ☐   Get rid of unsightly weeds and trash. If you have wood, lumber, or other items you simply must store in your yard, stack it neatly as much out of sight as possible. If you can afford it, put up lattice or other fencing as a screen. You could use shrubs, but if they aren't there already, they won't have time to grow.

3 ☐   A birdbath will add charm to your yard.

4 ☐   Create an inviting place for sitting or eating outdoors. You don't need expensive garden furniture to make it attractive. Inexpensive plastic will do. Pick colors that harmonize with the color of your house. Provide some shade for this area—put it under a tree or roof overhang, or provide an umbrella. You could put an attractive cloth on the table, and/or a potted flowering plant, weather permitting.

5 ☐   If your table and chairs are under a tree, you will need to wash them off frequently because of the birds.

6 ☐   If you are having an open house and the weather is warm, you might put a pitcher of lemonade and glasses or paper cups on the table in the shade. People will feel more at home—very important when considering buying a home.

7 ☐   The yard on the sides of your house should be taken care of as much as anywhere else.

8 ☐ Keep your garbage cans clean, lids on, and not overflowing.

9 ☐ If you have a swingset, keep it oiled. Otherwise, the noise is terrible. If it is rusted and unsightly, now is a good time to get rid of it. If your neighbors have a swingset that needs oiling and it drives you crazy, it will do the same to prospective buyers. Talk to your neighbors about it.

10 ☐ If your dog, or anyone else's dog, uses your yard for a bathroom, clean it up every day. If possible, talk with the dog's owner about it's using your yard. There is probably a leash law which you could tactfully refer to. As a last resort, you can call animal control. You might also need to spray the grass for fleas.

11 ☐ Fill in any area where water stands after rain with dirt to cut down on mosquitoes.

12 ☐ If your yard stinks from a faulty septic system, get it fixed.

13 ☐ A few flowering plants will add charm to your yard, especially around the sitting area.

14 ☐ Have something attractive in your yard to view from the kitchen window.

15 ☐ If the view from any window is incurably unsightly, hide it. You could install an 8-foot lattice screen near the fence if the unsightly view is your neighbor's yard. Or to draw the eye away from the view, you could paint the fence an attractive color which coordinates with your house. You could even paint a mural if you're artistic.

This works better for a small area, such as the side of the house. I wouldn't recommend it for your entire yard. A more expensive remedy would be to plant the tallest trees you can find available. They won't form a complete screen, but they will draw attention from the view, and promise a screen or the future.

16 ☐   Repair fences and decks if needed.

17 ☐   Tool sheds and other outbuildings should be cleaned up and put in order on the inside and painted on the outside. You may want to spray these areas if they are infested with spiders.

18 ☐   If you have a pool, keep it clean and free of algae. Repair cracks and faulty equipment.

19 ☐   Cracks in concrete patios can be treated with flower seeds, as suggested for the driveway in the section "At the Curb."

NOTES — THE BACKYARD

Pets

1 ☐   It's better from the standpoint of selling your home to board your pets at a neighbor's while your house is being shown, but you have to decide whether it will be too hard on your pet or your neighbor. If you keep them at home, take the steps below to minimize their impact on prospective buyers.

2 ☐   Keep your animals brushed and clean and dry. The smell of a wet dog, even a clean one, is not inviting to someone who doesn't have a dog.

3 ☐   Watch out for your cat. The only time my cat ever dragged something home was the day a couple who were very interested in buying my home brought their parents to look at it. We had a lovely home in the country, with a beautiful backyard and patio. They went out to look at the patio and there by the elegant French doors were a dead snake and a small bird with its head half-bitten off. Well, the women screamed and left in a hurry, and they didn't come back.

4 ☐   If you can't be home when the house is shown, take them with you or to a neighbor. Otherwise, keep your dogs in the basement or garage with a note on the door. If people are interested, they can make an appointment to see those areas when you are home. Even if your dog is friendly, he may be a distraction when someone is trying to look at your house.

5 ☐   Clean your cat's litter box every day. If you can, put the box in the garage or basement, *never* in the kitchen!

6 ☐   Clean bird and other animal cages every day. If the animals bite, put a warning note on the cage.

In General

1 ☐   Open curtains and blinds to make your rooms lighter, unless the view is unsightly. If you can't fix the view, leave blinds down but the slats open, or hang a semi-sheer curtain that lets in the light but not the view.

2 ☐   Clean your drapes and other window coverings. Repair or replace broken or torn ones. Clean your carpets. Clean your bedspreads. Air your pillows and mattresses in the sun for an hour or two if they smell musty.

3 ☐   Air out your house every day, even in the dead of winter. The smell of stale tobacco smoke can be a turn-off, even to smokers. Stale cooking odors and bathroom odors can pervade your whole house.

4 ☐   Changing or cleaning your furnace filter once a month will cut down on odors and dust.

5 ☐   Make sure you have no fleas, cockroaches, spiders, or other insects. Fumigate if you must.

If you have mice or rats, call the exterminator if you haven't already. Check around plumbing and heating pipes for small holes they could be entering through. They have soft bodies and can squeeze through holes smaller than they are. Stuff steel wool in the holes. Exterior doors and the garage entrance door may have spaces at the bottom if not weather stripped. You can get a do-it-yourself-kit at a hardware store. The instructions are on the package. It will keep your house warmer, too. Doggy doors, unfortunately, are a prime entry point. Perhaps it is time to replace the vinyl parts on yours. Can you shut it with a metal cover at night?

6 □   Mice don't usually hang around if you have a cat that spends time indoors. They are genetically programmed to be repelled by some chemical the cat exudes. This is about the extent of my scientific knowledge of the matter. I do know that I and my cat moved into a house with mice, and within a few days they were gone, never to return. There was no evidence my cat caught any of them. Dogs do not have the same effect on mice, and rats don't care who is in the house.

Notes — Pets and In General

What to Do if the House is Empty

An empty house will look less inviting than a tastefully decorated and lived-in one, but more inviting than a dirty, messy occupied one. All of the rules of cleanliness and neatness mentioned in the previous sections apply to empty houses as well. You can optimize its potential by doing a few additional things. Any cost incurred may be tax deductible from the selling price of the house. Check with your tax preparer. Every month that the house remains unsold, you're making another mortgage payment, so weigh this cost against what you would pay to get it sold faster.

1 ☐   If you can't maintain the yard yourself, hire a maintenance service.

2 ☐   Clean the house as needed. It will get dusty and the floors will get dirty from people traipsing through (we hope) to look at it.

3 ☐   Keep the electricity service on to provide more light, and keep the water on so the yard can be watered.

4 ☐   Window coverings should be just as attractive as if someone lived there.

5 ☐   If you can afford it, consider furnishing the living room, dining room and master bedroom—either rent or borrow furniture or use some of your own. For the entrance, a small chest or table with a vase of dried flowers or a large Oriental ginger jar would be a simple solution. In the empty bedrooms you could put a chair and side table or an easel with a picture on it. Maybe you can come up with a few ideas of your own.

6 ☐   In some areas, you can hire a caretaking service to provide reliable and neat live-in caretakers who specialize in properties for sale.

7 ☐   If animals have been living in the house, any fleas left behind can live for months without food and continue to produce offspring in warm weather. They will be very hungry when a human comes along, so a flea bomb after you move out is in order, even if you didn't think you had any fleas when you moved out.

LAST, BUT NOT LEAST

If you are going to be there when the house is shown:

1 ☐   Look as fresh and clean as your house. Don't wear your old painting clothes or hog-slopping overalls.

2 ☐   If you have an agent, let him or her do the showing and selling. Stay out of the way. Go out in the yard if they are looking in the house; go in the house if they are looking in the yard. Viewers may ask you questions. Don't lie, but don't offer extra information, even if you think it is positive. Your agent will provide the necessary information about your house and neighborhood. If you start conversing too freely, you may say something you'll regret.

3 ☐   Don't do noisy projects, such as mowing the lawn; keep music or television volume down or, better yet, off. Don't smoke or drink alcohol. Don't use foul language. In short, be on your best behavior. Send the children to a friend or neighbors. Why don't you go there, too.

Notes — What to Do if the House is Empty, and Last, But Not Least

___ _____

___ _____

___ _____

___ _____

___ _____

___ _____

___ _____

___ _____

___ _____

___ _____

___ _____

___ _____

___ _____

___ _____

___ _____

___ _____

TO DO LIST

——— _____

——— _____

——— _____

——— _____

——— _____

——— _____

——— _____

——— _____

——— _____

——— _____

——— _____

——— _____

——— _____

——— _____

——— _____

——— _____

——— _____

TO DO LIST

TO DO LIST

TO DO LIST

SHOPPING LIST

SHOPPING LIST

About the Author

A writer, editor, and veteran fixer-upper, Christina Vaughan has renovated residential homes and small apartment buildings for resale. Her observations when viewing properties prompted her to write this handy guide for home sellers, whether private sellers or real estate agents.

Visit our website to order more Guides and to see our children's interactive reading and drawing books recommended by educators.

www.castlebrookbooks.com

www.ingramcontent.com/pod-product-compliance
Lightning Source LLC
Chambersburg PA
CBHW071436200326
41520CB00014B/3715